HEROIN

Susan Elliot-Wright

Raintree

Chicago, Illinois

Design: Carole Binding
Photo research: Glass Onion Pictures

Library of Congress Cataloging-in-Publication Data:

Elliot-Wright, Susan.
 Heroin / Susan Elliot-Wright.
  p. cm. -- (Health issues)
Summary: Discusses the effects of heroin on the human body, the dangers of heroin abuse, and heroin abuse treatment and prevention.
Includes bibliographical references and index.
 ISBN 0-7398-6894-2 (lib. bdg.)
 1. Heroin habit--Juvenile literature. 2. Heroin--Juvenile literature.
3. Heroin--Physiological effect--Juvenile literature. [1. Heroin. 2. Drug abuse.] I. Title. II. Series.
 HV5822.H4E55 2005
 362.29'3--dc22

2003015746

1 2 3 4 5 6 7 8 9 0
07 06 05 04 03

Printed in China, bound in the United States

Acknowledgments

The author and publishers thank the following for their permission to reproduce photographs and illustrations: pp. 1, 17, 24, 27, 36, 47, 48 Rex Features; pp. 3, 30 Photofusion (Colin Edwards); pp. 5, 15, 21, 23, 49 (bottom), 54 Popperfoto.com; pp. 4, 33, 44, 45, 57, 59 Topham/ImageWorks; p. 7 Topham (Science Museum London/HIP); pp. 8, 11, 28 Topham Picturepoint; p. 13 Science Photo Library (Michael Donne); p. 19 Camera Press; p. 34 Science Photo Library (St Mary's Hospital Medical School); p. 37 Science Photo Library (Penny Tweedie); p. 39 Topham/Chapman; p. 41 Science Photo Library (Faye Norman); p. 43 Corbis Images (Lawrence Manning); p. 49 (top) Topham/PA; p. 50 Corbis Images (Chuck Savage); p. 52 Photofusion (Ulrike Preuss).

The illustrations on pages 25 and 29 are by Carole Binding.

Note: Photographs illustrating the case studies in this book were posed by models.

Cover photograph courtesy of Rex Features.

Every effort has been made to trace copyright holders. However, the publishers apologise for any unintentional omissions and would be pleased in such cases to add an acknowledgement in any future editions.

Contents

Introduction
What is Heroin?

You have probably heard a lot about heroin. You may already know that it is an extremely dangerous, illegal drug. Heroin has been classified as a "schedule 1" drug in the United States. This classification is given to the group of drugs that is considered to be the most dangerous. Anyone caught in possession of or selling one of these drugs faces serious penalties—up to life in prison.

Heroin is made from the juice of the opium poppy, which is refined into a powder. The powder is smoked, heated and inhaled, or dissolved and injected. It is highly addictive, can kill at first use, and often ruins the lives of those who become dependent on it. Heroin has been around for about 100 years, and its use has grown since the 1970s. This has led to serious drug problems in many parts of the world.

Raw opium
Cuts are made in the seedpod of an opium poppy, and its juice then oozes out. The juice is collected and can be processed into heroin powder.

Heroin use among celebrities, particularly those from the music world, has frequently hit the headlines. There have been stories of ruined lives and careers and heroin-linked deaths, such as that of Nirvana singer Kurt Cobain. But most heroin users are ordinary people who begin thinking they will "just try it once." There are currently an estimated 800,000 heroin users in the United States and 250,000 in the United Kingdom.

An average dependent user spends about $17,000 a year on his or her habit, and three-quarters of this money, according to recent government research, comes from crime. Many users end up in prison, homeless, jobless, in poor health, and with no contact with their families. About a third will die as a result of heroin use. Chapter 4 looks at what heroin can do to someone's body, and chapter 5 looks more at what happens to the life of the user.

Addicted
Many heroin users inject the drug. It is highly addictive, and addiction develops quickly. Obtaining and taking heroin become the focus of the person's life.

Why, you might wonder, if heroin is so terrible, does anybody use it at all? When heroin is first used, it gives the user a powerful, sudden sense of pleasure and well-being, a feeling described as a "high," or "rush." Chapter 3 explains the effect heroin has on the brain to cause this sensation and make the person associate heroin with extreme pleasure. It is often people who live in unhappy or underprivileged circumstances who are most attracted to drugs, seeing them as a way to escape the pain of their lives. The sad fact is that the pleasure heroin gives evaporates quickly and the original pain returns, with the addition of unpleasant withdrawal symptoms that only disappear (temporarily) with more heroin. This is how addiction begins.

In recent years, much of the discussion in schools about drugs has focused on marijuana and so-called "clubbing" drugs such as ecstasy. Some experts fear that this has resulted in today's young people not being aware of the dangers of heroin. Chapter 6 addresses the issue of education and information and asks whether better drug education would help reduce the number of people becoming addicted.

"We talk about drugs at school, but I don't know that much about heroin. I read about it in the papers sometimes, and it sounds scary."
(Charlie, age 15)

Depending on where you live, you may be aware of drug treatment or rehabilitation centers in your area. You may even know someone who is dependent on heroin, or who has tried it. It is often the case that, when somebody has a problem with drugs or alcohol, they are unable to see that problem clearly for themselves. This may mean that what they say about a certain drug, or a particular aspect of drug use, is less than accurate. The purpose of this book is to provide straightforward information about heroin and its effects on the individual and on society. Hopefully, it will answer any questions you may have and clear up some of the myths about heroin use.

Help

If you need more information about heroin, or if you know someone who might need help, the organizations listed on page 62 may be useful.

1 Heroin's Forerunners
A Brief History of Opiates

Heroin is one of a group of drugs called opiates. The name "opiate" comes from the opium poppy, that grows across central and southeast Asia. The seedpod of the poppy produces a sticky substance called opium, which has been widely used both recreationally and as a medicine for centuries. Opiates, including heroin, morphine, and codeine, are derived from opium. There are also synthetic (human-made) opiates, such as Demerol and methadone.

The use of opium in ancient civilizations

The first records of the use of opium as a painkiller, or analgesic, date back 6,000 years to the Sumerians. They referred to the opium poppy as "the joy plant." Ancient Egyptian and Babylonian writings also contain references to opium preparations for the relief of pain and to an accompanying sense of well-being and calm. These ancient peoples either ate parts of the flower or made them into a drink.

Opium use in China

In about the 7th or 8th century C.E., Arab traders introduced opium to China, where it continued to be used as a medicine, but where recreational use began to grow steadily. Around this time it was discovered that igniting and smoking the opium produced a more powerful effect, and the habit of opium smoking spread. Opium pipes became a sort of fashion accessory, ranging from plain clay or bamboo pipes to elaborately decorated and bejeweled creations called "hookahs." The type of pipe would reflect the wealth of the user.

Opium pipe
This Chinese pipe for smoking opium was made from ivory, with an ornate metal mount.

Opium makes users sleepy, lethargic, and uninterested in the world around them. It reduces the desire and ability to work, study, maintain relationships, or have sex. The desire to eat may disappear, and, even if it does not, the body's ability to digest food is weakened. Long-term use of opium impairs many of the body's physical and psychological functions. Opium is also highly addictive, which means that once people start to use it regularly, they may find it extremely difficult to stop. At first, this is because the drug gives them a good feeling, but eventually they take it because if they don't, they start to suffer unpleasant "withdrawal symptoms."

Western doctors working in China at the end of the 19th century reported that opium was "a ruinous drug." One is quoted as saying, "It destroys morals, makes physical wrecks, and severs social relationships." Around this time in China, an estimated 70,000 or 80,000 opium addicts were dying yearly. The effect on Chinese society was devastating. In order to finance their addiction, male opium users would sell everything—sometimes even their wives and children. When everything was gone, they would turn to begging and stealing. Women addicts often resorted to prostitution.

Physical wrecks
This photograph of opium smokers in China shows how opium took over the lives of users, often at the expense of their health.

The Chinese Opium wars

Until the 18th century, trade between Britain and China was mostly in China's favor. The Chinese sold tea, which had become fashionable in Europe, as well as beautiful silk and porcelain, but they had little interest in buying what they regarded as inferior British products. Then the British began to export opium from India, at that time a British colony, to China. Opium became popular as a recreational drug, and addiction began to ravage parts of China, especially around Canton (now known as Guangzhou), where most overseas trade took place. Britain's opium exports to China resulted in two wars.

The First Opium War, 1839–1842

In 1839 Lin Ze-xu, a Chinese government official, was appointed to stamp out the opium trade. He wrote to Queen Victoria, asking her to stop Britain's merchants from trafficking "this poisonous drug." The queen ignored him. He then demanded that the traders hand over their opium stocks, but they held off for six weeks before finally giving up more than 20,000 barrels of opium, which was then destroyed. Lin Ze-xu refused to allow the traders to buy tea, rice, or silk for export until they signed a pledge promising not to bring any more opium into the country. This sparked an aggressive response from British opium traders and the British military, which landed on and occupied Hong Kong. The antiquated Chinese army and navy were no match for the British military, and China was defeated. The war ended in 1842 with the Treaty of Nanking, which not only gave the British trading rights in five ports, but also gave control of Hong Kong to "her Britannic Majesty, her heirs, and successors." (Control of Hong Kong was returned to the Chinese in 1997.)

The Second Opium War, 1856–1860

In 1856 the British wanted to extend trading rights and attacked China again. The Chinese were defeated and forced to sign the treaties of Tientsin (1858), which opened up more ports to Western trade and residence and provided freedom of movement for Christian missionaries. Further negotiations led to legalizing the importation of opium. At first the Chinese refused to comply, but after Peking (now Beijing) was captured and the emperor's summer palace burned down, they signed the Peking Convention (1860), agreeing to observe the treaties of Tientsin.

Opium use in the West

In the West, opium use became a widespread problem in the 19th century. "Opium dens," where people could go to smoke opium, became popular in Europe and the United States, especially in areas with established Chinese communities. One of the main problems was the use of opium in medicines. Opium-related preparations were used for a variety of ailments, including tuberculosis, malaria, and diarrhea. Many "over-the-counter" medicines contained opium or morphine. With names such as "Mrs. Winslow's Soothing Syrup," "Ayer's Cherry Pectoral," and "Atkinson's Royal Infant Preservative," they sounded harmless enough and were advertised as "cough mixtures," "painkillers," and "women's friends." People at the time did not realize that something that could "cure" could actually be harmful.

Laudanum: A Victorian cure-all

Laudanum was a mixture of opium, alcohol, and spices. It was originally thought of as a "working-class" drug because it was very cheap, but it soon became popular across all levels of Victorian society. Like the various medicines

Babies and children on drugs

In the 19th century, nannies, nursemaids, and exhausted mothers calmed restless and crying babies by giving them spoonsful of laudanum to help them sleep. Sales of "Godfrey's Cordial," an opium-based colic remedy, were high. One druggist in the north of England admitted to selling half a gallon each week. Another sold 400 gallons of laudanum annually.

"Poppy tea" was also given to children in some parts of England, and doctors noted how infants in those areas seemed "shrank up into little old men" or "wizened like monkeys." Many babies died as a result of overdose, and more still died of starvation. A doctor investigating the high infant mortality rate noted how children "kept in a state of continuous narcotism will be thereby disinclined for food." Death from malnutrition was likely to result.

containing opium, both laudanum and raw opium were easy to buy at pharmacies and grocery stores. Some doctors prescribed laudanum for headaches, sleeplessness, or depression, often dispensing the drug themselves. Many upper-class Victorian ladies became increasingly dependent on laudanum to relieve the stress and boredom of their daily lives.

Sharpening the senses

Laudanum was also widely used in artistic circles, particularly by writers and poets who felt that it sharpened the senses and made them more creative. Charles Dickens, Samuel Taylor Coleridge, and Lord Byron were known to be users. Lewis Carroll was said to go to opium dens, and he may well have written *Alice in Wonderland* under the influence of laudanum. The dreamlike world in which Alice exists certainly suggests a drug-induced state, and the book may even refer to smoking opium:

"She peeped over the edge of the mushroom, and her eyes immediately met those of a large blue caterpillar that was sitting on the top, with its arms folded, quietly smoking a long hookah, and taking not the smallest notice of anything else."

The blue caterpillar
The sleepy, laid-back state of this character in Alice in Wonderland *sounds similar to the state of someone smoking opium.*

Thomas De Quincey (1785–1859), the author of *Confessions of an English Opium Eater* (1821), gives some clue as to why the drug was so popular:

" . . . The opium eater . . . feels that the diviner part of his nature is paramount; that is, the moral affections are in a state of cloudless serenity; and over all is the light of the majestic intellect."

But people soon became addicted to the drug, partly because the body quickly developed a tolerance to it. This means it required more each time to get the same effect. Writer Wilkie Collins (1824–1889) used laudanum to kill the intense pain he suffered as a result of rheumatic gout. He carried around a silver flask of laudanum from which he needed to drink ever-increasing amounts in order to gain relief. By the end of his life, according to his doctor, Sir William Fergusson, he was consuming enough each day to kill twelve people. Although this may well have been an exaggeration, it is probably accurate to say that, over the years, his body had built up such a tolerance that it was able to stand amounts that would certainly have killed someone who was not used to those quantities. People who die from opiate abuse usually die of organ failure, often failure of the heart or lungs.

Morphine

Today, the use of raw opium has almost disappeared in the West. Drug manufacturers convert most opium into the legal painkiller codeine, although large quantities of morphine, a more powerful analgesic, are also produced.

Morphine was first separated from opium by a German pharmacist in 1805. He named it after Morpheus, the Greek god of dreams. Morphine is used legally to treat severe pain such as that experienced after an operation, but a side effect of its painkilling action is a feeling of detachment and euphoria. The drug is also highly addictive. Morphine is not usually imported illegally, but addicts do frequently steal it

Essential medication
Morphine is an important painkilling drug used in hospitals.

from hospitals. Ironically, before its addictive nature became known, morphine was often given to treat opium addiction and alcoholism. The idea was that the morphine would relieve the withdrawal symptoms experienced when the person stopped taking the substance to which they were addicted. Then, once the person's body had become used to not receiving the addictive substance, the morphine could be stopped. Even when it was realized that morphine itself was addictive, the treatment was still used because morphine was thought to be less harmful to the body than opium.

Fact file

In China at the start of the 20th century, Christian missionaries handed out morphine pills as remedies for opium addiction. In fact, the pills were used recreationally as a substitute for opium and soon became known as "Jesus-Opium."

Synthetic opiates

These are human-made painkiller drugs that act similarly to opium-derived drugs. For example, Demerol, like morphine or heroin, produces a "rush"—a sense of instant euphoria—immediately after it is taken, usually by injection. Because this feeling of well-being is so desirable, recreational users are eager to repeat the experience. This cycle often leads to addiction. Methadone is another synthetic opiate. It can also produce a rush when injected, but it is not as strong. Its painkilling effects can last for up to 12 hours.

Tolerance to synthetic opiates develops quickly, and the power of the rush or "hit" quickly diminishes. But tolerance is lost again fairly quickly, so there is a strong risk of overdose.

When the hypodermic syringe was developed in the mid-19th century, people began to inject pure morphine. It was mistakenly thought that injecting was not as addictive as swallowing morphine pills. Use of the drug as a legal medicine to treat wounded servicemen during the Civil War (1861–1865) led to extremely high levels of addiction, which became known as "the soldiers' disease." A hundred years later, soldiers fighting in the Vietnam War also became addicted.

Heroin: a cure for morphine addiction

Heroin was originally developed toward the end of the 19th century as a treatment for addiction to morphine. It is made by adding chemicals to morphine, making it more easily absorbed by the body. Heroin was thought to be a safe and non-addictive alternative. In fact, it is at least as addictive as morphine and has become known as one of the most dangerous and destructive drugs available today.

2 Heroin Use Today
Supply and Demand

By the time heroin, sometimes known as Smack, H, Skag, Horse, or Junk, reaches our streets, it is in the form of a white or brownish powder. It is usually sold in a "bag" containing a single dose, or "hit." Pure heroin is white, but this is rarely sold on the street. Most street heroin varies from off-white to dark brown because of impurities left from the manufacturing process or because of the presence of additives.

Street heroin is often mixed, or "cut," with other substances, including anything from sugar or powdered milk to scouring powder, brick dust, glass, or rat poison. Traditionally, the purity of heroin in a bag ranged from 1 to 10 percent. More recently, as the cost of buying heroin in bulk has fallen, dealers have been able to make their profit without using large quantities of additives. This means that the purity of heroin in a wrap may now be as high as 98 percent.

It is impossible for users to know exactly what they are buying or the strength of the heroin they are getting. If they think they have established a "safe" dose but then one day take heroin that is much purer than what they are used to, the result will be overdose and, possibly, death.

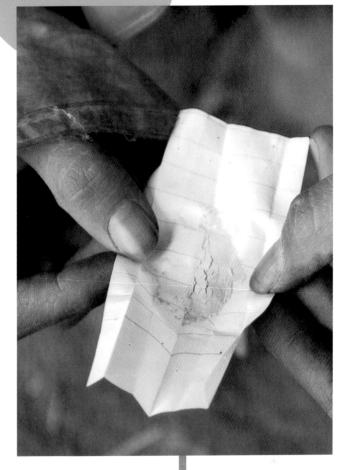

A heroin bag
Heroin users normally buy the drug in single doses. The amount of the powder that is actually heroin varies.

Heroin slang

Junkie—*heroin addict*

Shooting up—*injecting heroin*

Chasing the dragon—*heating heroin and inhaling the vapors produced*

Cut—*to mix, or "bulk," heroin with another substance in order to increase profit*

Cooking up—*preparing heroin for injection*

Works—*name for the paraphernalia associated with injecting*

Clean—*having gotten off heroin*

There are several ways to take heroin. The powder can be snorted, smoked, heated on foil and inhaled (known as "chasing the dragon"), or mixed with water, heated, and then injected. Another form, "black-tar heroin," which is manufactured mainly in Mexico, has become increasingly available in the United States. It looks just like it sounds— black and sticky, like roofing tar. It is usually dissolved, diluted, and injected.

What's the attraction?

Heroin is a fast-acting drug that affects the brain's pleasure center (read more about this in Chapter 4), producing a "rush"—a surge of pleasure that may be accompanied by a warm, contented feeling, a detachment from the "real world," and relief from anxiety. The effects depend on how the drug is taken. Injection produces the most intense response most quickly—usually within a few seconds.

On the down side, users, especially those using the drug for the first time, may experience nausea and vomiting. Speech may be slurred, the eyelids may droop, and the user may suffer chronic constipation. Repeated use has devastating consequences, both to health and to everyday life. The drug is viciously addictive, and addiction develops quickly. Since the need for the drug becomes the most important thing in their life, many users turn to crime in order to finance their habit. Heroin addicts often end up with no job or home, and they may be reduced to begging on the streets. About 2 percent of users who inject the drug die each year.

How does heroin end up on our streets?

Much of the world's heroin—75 percent—comes from Afghanistan. The other main sources are Pakistan, Mexico, and, more recently, Colombia, which is the main source of heroin entering the United States. The length of the "heroin chain"—the chain of people involved in bringing heroin to our streets—can vary. It may have as few as five links: opium farmer-manufacturer-importer-dealer-user.

Heroin production begins with the farming of opium poppies. The farmer collects raw opium by making cuts in the pod of the poppy. Over the next few days, the sticky opium oozes out of the cuts, and each morning, the farmer scrapes this off. Farmers usually then sell their raw opium at local markets to opium traders, or they may carry out the next stage themselves.

Afghanistan

Until 2000 it was legal for farmers in Afghanistan to grow and sell their opium. In 2000 cultivation (growing) of opium poppies became illegal, but trading in opium was still permitted. In 2002 trading in opium was also banned, although it still continues on a large scale.

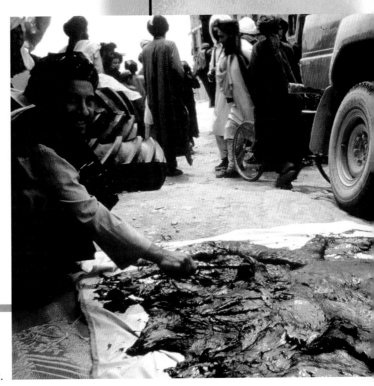

Opium for sale

This farmer is displaying the raw opium he has for sale at a local market in Afghanistan.

This next stage is processing. It is carried out by the farmers or local traders in makeshift laboratories, using basic techniques and equipment. The raw opium is converted into morphine base by dissolving it in boiling water, adding lime (a white substance used in making cement and sometimes as a fertilizer), filtering, then adding concentrated ammonia before heating again. The morphine solidifies and settles at the bottom of the pot. It is then wrapped into blocks and dried in the sun before being sold to manufacturers with slightly more sophisticated laboratories, where it is further refined. The base is heated and simple chemicals such as acetic acid are added. Finally, sodium carbonate, a common ingredient in soap, is added to form heroin base.

"Smoking heroin" is made by mixing heroin base with hydrochloric acid and addictive substances such as caffeine. The resulting paste dries into brownish lumps that are crushed before being sold. This heroin, sometimes known as "brown sugar" due to its appearance, is around 20 to 30 percent pure.

The white powder that is suitable for injection is made by adding hydrochloric acid and ether to the heroin base. It is then filtered, dried, and compressed into bricks. This heroin has a purity of 80 to 90 percent.

"It all comes down to greed. All along the chain, the price goes up, with everyone making a fat profit—except for the poor people who grow the stuff and the kids who die on the street after taking it."
(Andy Willis, "Drug Squad" detective)

Manufacturers in Afghanistan may sell their heroin to brokers, who ship it to importers in destination countries. These brokers often recruit couriers, sometimes called "mules," to carry heroin in small amounts. Large quantities enter the destination countries by various routes, smuggled in among legitimate imported goods or hidden in luggage, boats, cars, and trucks. Midlevel distributors then purchase the drug. At this point, it may be bulked out with cutting agents and sold to street-level dealers. By the time it gets to the user, the heroin costs about 60 times more than the farmer was paid for it.

Heroin haul

Customs officers seized these portions of heroin wrapped in latex. People recruited by drug smugglers to carry them from one country to another would have swallowed them.

Drug smugglers

Drug smugglers are constantly looking for new ways to get heroin through customs. "Mules," or "body packers," can carry large quantities either in suitcases or in their stomachs—in latex balloons that they swallow before boarding a plane. Upon arrival, they retrieve the heroin by making themselves vomit or by taking laxatives and passing it out via the bowel.

In many cases, the smuggled heroin is discovered when the "mule" becomes ill due to heroin leaking into the stomach. Often "mules" have been rushed to the hospital with stomach pains, only to be arrested after an X ray or surgery reveals the hidden drug. Many have died after the package has burst, flooding their system with heroin and causing a fatal overdose.

In March 2003, a man was arrested for trying to smuggle 40 pounds (18 kilograms) of highly refined heroin, worth more than $6 million, into India. It was hidden in almond shells.

Heroin is bought on the street by users, who may buy more than they need in order to sell some for a small profit to help fund their own habit. The cost of a single dose of heroin has fallen considerably due to the increased availability. Heroin can now be found for as little as $17 a bag.

It has often been suggested that a dealer will "push" heroin—that is, give away a "free sample." The idea is that the person will enjoy the free hit so much that he or she will be eager to try again and will buy the next dose, quickly becoming addicted and providing the dealer with a new customer. Some drug organizations say that this is a myth, claiming that one hit does not guarantee addiction and that "free trials" are only given between dealers and users who have built up a relationship over some time.

When is heroin not heroin?

In 2002 a British journalist went out on the streets in various cities to see what drugs were available and what they cost. When the heroin he purchased was analyzed, it was found that the amount and purity varied enormously from place to place. One bag of heroin actually contained .4 ounces—less than one-half of an ounce. Some "heroin" was in fact mainly pulverized stone and glass.

"I started dealing"

"I was on H for years, and I was always obsessed with how I was going to afford the next hit. I sold everything I owned, and a lot of what other people owned, too. I even stole stuff from my grandma. Eventually, I started dealing. Only small amounts—I couldn't afford to buy a lot at one time. But it was a good way to increase my income.

"I knew some of the stuff I bought was cut with other things—sometimes it was glucose or flour, other times it could be talcum powder, cleaning agents, or brick dust. People sometimes ask me if I ever worry about what that junk might have done to the guys who used it, and yeah, I do worry about it now. But at the time, all you care about is the next hit. The kid could fall down and die in front of you, and you wouldn't care—as long as he'd paid you up front, of course."
(Tony, age 23, ex–heroin user)

A lethal crop

You might wonder why farmers continue to grow opium that they know will be made into heroin. The reason is that they can earn far more by growing opium than by growing other crops, although their earnings are still fairly low.

In July 2000 the growing of opium poppies was banned in Afghanistan under the Taliban government. As a result, the production of opium fell to 204 tons (185 metric tonnes) in 2001. However, because of the smaller quantities available, the price of heroin shot up. Opium farmers received little compensation for their lost livelihood, and many were close to ruin. With no incentive to observe the ban, many replanted their fields to take advantage of the higher prices. The result was a bumper crop—about 3,900 tons (3,500 metric tonnes)—in 2002, leading to a fall in prices and a flood of high-quality heroin on the streets.

"I picked coffee beans for a living, but the price kept falling and in the end there was no work. I have a wife and five children to feed. With poppies I can make a living. I can even save a little."
(Tehru Akran, Afghan opium farmer)

Destroying heroin

In July 2002, as a sign of their determination to crack down on the drug trade, the authorities in Afghanistan lit a bonfire of refined opium that had been seized from local traders.

3 Why Do People Use Heroin? The Slippery Slope of Addiction

Young people try drugs for a number of reasons, but the most common is curiosity: "What will happen if I take this?" "How will it make me feel?" In a British survey on this subject in spring 2002, 75 percent of those taking part cited curiosity as the main reason they had tried illegal drugs, with 22 percent blaming peer pressure, and 3 percent a "desire to emulate heroes." The vast majority of people who try a drug do not become long-term users.

"I know these guys who smoke heroin and I must admit, I'm tempted just to find out what it feels like. I think I'd be too scared to try it, though." (Fin, age 15)

Many drugs produce a sense of euphoria, an intense feeling of pleasure and general well-being sometimes described as being "high." Some drugs make users feel more relaxed, others make users feel lively, confident, and full of energy. But what all addictive drugs have in common is that the feeling of pleasure is soon followed by the opposite feeling. The user begins to "come down," often experiencing extreme tiredness, depression, or deeply unpleasant physical symptoms. With heroin, the "high" is sudden, sometimes described as a "rush" of pleasure. Users talk of a feeling of escape, of complete, worry-free detachment. But coming down can be devastating; the high is followed by a "crash."

Heroin culture

The story of Becky, on page 23, is typical of many heroin users: an unhappy home life, running away to a big city, and feeling lonely and vulnerable. Young people who end up sleeping on the streets often find themselves part of a group that may include people who abuse heroin and other drugs. Heroin offers an immediate sense of well-being and escape from real life, including problems. For this reason, it is often people who are already on the edge of society who are attracted to the drug—for example, criminals, those without jobs or homes, or those suffering from depression or other mental-health problems. As a result, heroin users, linked by a feeling of being outside of society, soon form friendships among themselves.

The shared obsession with finding the next fix means they are all "in the same boat," and this leads to a sense of bonding and belonging. Other users become a substitute for family and

"Something special"

"I used to live in a house, once, with my parents. It was only three years ago, but it seems much longer. I ran away from home after a fight with my mom's boyfriend. They asked me to come back, but they didn't really want me. I've never gotten along with my parents, but things just got worse. Anyway, I wanted to prove I didn't need them.

"I'd smoked some weed before, but then I met a guy who said that weed was for kids, and that if I wanted something really special, he could arrange it. So I tried heroin. You're told it's a killer—the worst thing you can do. So it attracts you all the more. I only wanted to try it once, partly to see what it was like, partly just to do something dangerous. Also, I thought it would be cool. Now look at me. I used to think I'd get married one day, perhaps have kids, but no one would come near me now. I've got friends on the street—well, they're not friends, really. We shoot up together, but if I died, they wouldn't really care—probably wouldn't even notice. I might get AIDS. Might already have it, for all I know. I don't think about the future anymore. My last fix was five hours ago, so I'll need more soon. That's my future."
(Becky, age 19)

Friendship?
A shared need for heroin brings people together.

friends, and daily life becomes a constant challenge to find money for heroin. Days may consist of begging, stealing, or prostitution in order to fund the habit. With no worthwhile occupation and so little social contact, users may find comfort in the rituals of buying heroin and preparing it for injection. Addicts may become almost as dependent on the rituals as on the drug itself.

Petty thieving

Often the motive for stealing is that the object taken can be sold, providing money to buy heroin or other drugs.

One thing leads to another

Some drugs—marijuana, for example—are often seen by young people as "soft" drugs that will not do them any harm. Indeed, there are many people who believe that using such drugs should not be a criminal offense. However, many who have come into contact with the horror of heroin addiction, or have experienced it themselves, argue that so-called soft drugs can put users on the path to more dangerous drugs because they seek increasingly strong mind-altering effects. It could be that using marijuana involves people in buying illegal drugs, making it more likely that they will be offered heroin at some point. Drug organizations agree that almost all heroin users have used marijuana. However, only a small proportion of those who use marijuana go on to use heroin.

How addiction works

Addiction is defined by the medical profession as "the repeated compulsive use of a substance despite unpleasant or even life-threatening consequences." Experts still do not know as much as they would like about the nature of addiction, since there is little research on the subject, but they agree that it usually involves both physical and psychological dependence.

Psychological dependence

Heroin mimics the action of endorphins, which are chemicals that occur naturally in the brain. Endorphins are the body's natural "feel good" chemicals. They block pain and induce feelings of pleasure and well-being. The brain produces these chemicals in larger quantities when we do something enjoyable, such as play our favorite sports, go dancing, or laugh—the natural "highs" of daily life. When these highs occur, or when pain is relieved, the endorphins stimulate the production of another chemical called dopamine, which creates vivid, positive memories of the experience.

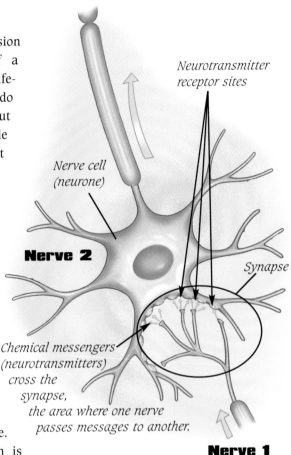

Neurotransmitter receptor sites

Nerve cell (neurone)

Nerve 2

Synapse

Chemical messengers (neurotransmitters) cross the synapse, the area where one nerve passes messages to another.

Nerve 1

Dopamine acts as a sort of messenger, telling another part of the brain, "the reward center," that you feel great. When users take heroin, much more dopamine is released than would occur due to the action of natural endorphins. The users' brains feel intense pleasure during the rush of the heroin hit and soon begin to associate taking heroin with feeling great. Taking heroin quickly becomes an experience users are eager to repeat.

Physical dependence

Before long, the body gets used to heroin. This is called tolerance. The brain begins to adapt to the over-stimulation of dopamine, and users need more and more

Chemical messengers

Nerves in the brain communicate with each other by passing tiny amounts of chemicals between the end of one nerve and the beginning of the next. The result of taking heroin is that a very large amount of the chemical messenger, or neurotransmitter, called dopamine is produced, and this increases the brain's activity.

heroin in order to get the same "high." In addition, users' brains become less sensitive to natural endorphins, so unless they take heroin, the brain will not release enough dopamine. As a result, users are likely to experience feelings of anxiety and despair, and so they take more heroin to relieve those feelings. Very soon, they no longer experience the pleasure that they associate with heroin; they are taking it purely to get rid of the bad feelings—called "withdrawal symptoms"—that are generated by its use. By this time, they need heroin in order to feel normal. They are now addicted.

Withdrawal symptoms

Withdrawal symptoms can occur within hours of the last use of heroin, although they are usually at their worst between 48 and 72 hours after last use. After this, they begin to ease off over several days. The symptoms include:

- *intense craving for heroin*
- *anxiety*
- *restlessness*
- *insomnia*

- *fever and sweating*
- *aching limbs and painful cramps*
- *vomiting and diarrhea*
- *chills and shivering*

How fast do people become addicted?

Experts suggest that daily heroin use over six to eight weeks is likely to lead to dependence. It varies, however, depending on a number of factors, including physical makeup, state of mind, and social situation. People differ in their sensitivity to all drugs, including alcohol; for instance, some are "social drinkers" throughout their lives, while others become alcoholics or "alcohol-dependent." There is no way of knowing in advance how someone may react to any drug, but addicts almost always say that they did not realize they were becoming addicted until it was too late.

"I never thought it could happen to me"

Matt was studying medicine when he started using heroin. His father was a doctor, and Matt had dreams of becoming a heart surgeon. According to his teachers, he was one of their brightest students. But he was thrown out of medical school in his third year, after becoming addicted to heroin. After living on the streets for awhile, he now lives with his family again, but he is still fighting his addiction.

"I never thought it could happen to me," says Matt. "The first time, I was at a party with a girl in my class. She said that 'chasing the dragon' was safe, and that I'd feel better than I'd ever felt in my life. Well, it didn't feel as great as I thought, and I threw up. But I was intrigued enough to try again, and that time, it was fantastic, incredible. So then I thought, well, I don't spend my money on fancy clothes or anything, so why not? Just at weekends and parties. But after the first few times, it wasn't as good as before, and I was feeing really bad in between, so I started using it more often. At that point, I was still going to classes. But then even twice a day wasn't helping, and that's when I started injecting. In the end, they threw me out of college. I don't know whether it was because of the heroin or whether it was the stealing—I had to steal stuff because my parents wouldn't give me any more money. I stayed with friends for awhile, but most of the time I was sleeping badly. I'm back home now, but I don't know how long I'll stay. It's harder to get a fix down here, and although my parents have been supportive, I know it hurts them to see me like this."

Who uses heroin?

Most heroin users first try it in between the ages of 18 and 21. Unfortunately, that age may be becoming lower. A 1999 National Institutes of Health study showed that more than 2 percent of eighth graders clamed to have tried heroin. This is two times the rate reported in 1991.

Traditionally, heroin use has been associated with deprived areas of towns and cities. Although studies show that its use is still more prevalent in poorer areas, there is some evidence to suggest that heroin use is increasing in rural areas and across different social groups. One of the reasons for this is possibly the fact that, due to the large crops of opium available in recent years, street heroin is increasing in purity and falling in price. This means that better-quality heroin is available to more people.

Also, the fashion for "chasing the dragon"—inhaling the vapor from heated heroin— means that it is not necessary to inject the drug. People can use heroin without the health risks associated with injecting, such as HIV and hepatitis (see chapter 4). However, many people try inhaling or smoking heroin after wrongly assuming, that these methods will not lead to addiction. This is ironic because in the 19th century morphine users actually switched to injecting morphine, believing that injecting would not lead to addiction.

Chasing the dragon

Heating heroin and inhaling the fumes is no less addictive than injecting the drug.

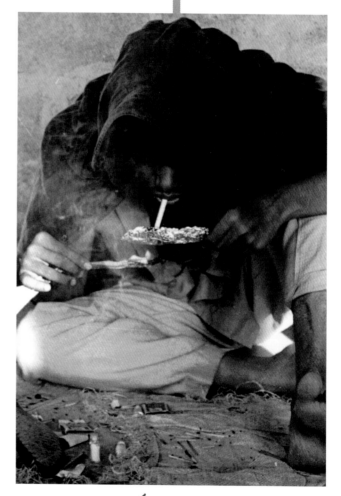

4 How Heroin Damages Health
A Powerful Poison

What does heroin do to the user's body?

Heroin enters the user's bloodstream—directly, if it is injected, or via the lungs, if it is smoked or inhaled. It then crosses the "blood-brain barrier," getting into the brain within 30 seconds. Like all opiates, heroin has a depressant effect on the central nervous system, the system consisting of the brain and spinal cord. This is why opiates work as painkillers: They depress the nerve transmissions that signal pain.

Blood vessel supplying brain

Many substances cannot pass through vessel wall

Tightly packed layer of cells

Heroin particles can pass through into brain

Passing through

The blood vessels that supply the brain are lined with cells that prevent many substances in the blood from crossing into the brain. But this lining is not a barrier for heroin.

Heroin and the blood-brain barrier

Heroin enters the brain very quickly because it is able to cross what is known as the "blood-brain barrier." The tiny blood vessels, or capillaries, that supply the brain are lined with a tightly packed layer of cells that act as a barrier preventing many substances from crossing into the brain and causing damage. But heroin dissolves in the blood's fatty acids, and this enables it to pass through the barrier.

Heroin works by attaching to sites called "opioid receptors," which are part of the body's mechanism for feeling pleasure and relieving pain. These receptors exist because the body produces its own natural chemicals, called endorphins, to kill pain, promote pleasure, control mood, and cope with stress. When heroin is taken, the receptors are bombarded, so that the brain's "pleasure center" is stimulated to an unnatural degree.

Although heroin stimulates the pleasure center, it has the opposite (slowing-down) effect on other systems in the body, such as the respiratory, cardiovascular (controlling the heart and circulation), and digestive systems. It causes a drop in body temperature and slows down breathing so that, after the first euphoric rush, the muscles relax, the limbs feel heavy, and the eyelids droop. The user is likely to feel very drowsy, a condition sometimes called "nodding off," and may feel confused and disorientated. The heart beats much more slowly and weakly and so blood is not circulated properly. In an overdose, breathing may actually stop, and the user dies. Heroin suppresses the digestive system, causing loss of appetite and constipation, which can be severe. Heroin also affects the concentration of hormones in the body, causing irregular periods in women and loss of sexual desire in both sexes.

System slow-down

Heroin slows down all the systems of the body. An overdose can lead to death.

Short-term problems

The first time people use heroin, they may vomit or experience severe nausea and dizziness. If they use a needle that has already been used by someone else, there is also the risk of catching infections such as HIV or hepatitis.

Overdose, which may be fatal, is possible at first use, although it is more common in long-term users whose tolerance has decreased as a result of not taking heroin for awhile—for example, if they have been in prison or have been trying to get off the drug. Overdose is also more

Dead in a public bathroom

"Adam was a normal boy. He'd just left school and started to work in a music store. It wasn't a wonderful job, but he seemed to like it. He made lots of friends, went to lots of parties— I was pleased that he was enjoying himself.

"I had no idea he was into drugs until he started stealing from me, taking money out of my purse, things from the house, and so on. In the end, he admitted that it was for heroin. He said he didn't know the drug was heroin when he first tried it—the girl who gave it to him called it something different, and it wasn't in a syringe. I think they smoked it or inhaled it or something.

"Anyway, Adam promised he'd try to get off it, and we—his father and I—said we'd help as much as we could. We made an appointment with our doctor so that we could try to find a rehabilitation program for him, and the three of us had an appointment on a Monday morning. But on the Saturday before, Adam went out with some friends and never came home again. As soon as the doobell rang, I knew he was dead. A policeman came to tell us. Adam had been found dead in a public bathroom. What an awful place to die."
(Sheila, whose son died of a heroin overdose at age 18)

common in those who inject and those who have other drugs, including alcohol, in their bloodstream. Most heroin users use a variety of other drugs.

When people overdose on heroin, they fall into what may appear to be a deep sleep, followed by a coma. Friends often assume they will "sleep it off" and be okay in the morning, but if they do not receive medical attention quickly, the coma may be followed by death. In some cases, death from heroin use occurs because the person vomits while unconscious and inhales some of the vomit. This causes asphyxiation, suffocation due to blockage of the airways that bring oxygen to the lungs.

Additives

In addition to these risks, street heroin may be mixed with various substances, any one of which may be a poison itself. Many of the additives in street heroin, which can include powdered glass or brick dust, do not dissolve in the blood. Eventually they may clog the blood vessels that lead to the lungs, liver, kidneys, or brain, and the result of this can be infection, the death of small patches of cells when blood flow to vital organs is seriously restricted, or even the death of the user.

Effects of long-term use

Once people start using heroin regularly, they are highly likely to become addicted. The more heroin they use, the more the body adjusts to the dose, and as the body's tolerance increases, they will need to take ever higher doses in order to achieve the same effect. Gradually, the "high," or "rush," diminishes and withdrawal symptoms, which can only be relieved by another "fix," or "hit," of the drug, kick in. Eventually, users no longer experience the euphoria that first made heroin attractive; they are now merely taking the drug in order to feel normal.

One of the major problems of heroin addiction is that it takes over users' lives. People become so dependent on heroin that finding the next dose—and the means to pay for it—becomes the sole purpose in life. This can lead to a complete lack of interest in personal well-being and may result in poor hygiene, inadequate diet, and general ill-health. In addition, users may turn to crime in order to pay for the habit (read more about this in Chapter 5).

Long-term heroin users are also more prone to depression and anxiety and, from an Australian study published in 2002, fourteen times more likely than their peers to take their own lives. It is not clear whether this is the result of the drug itself or of other factors, such as the lifestyle of the user, or social or psychological problems that may have contributed to the person turning to drugs in the first place.

Other health risks
Breathing problems

Respiratory (breathing) problems are common in heroin users. These are conditions that affect the lungs, such as pneumonia, asthma, and tuberculosis. Reasons for this may be the depressant effects of heroin on the respiratory system, the fact that blood vessels leading to the lungs are clogged with the additives in the heroin taken, and/or the poor health of the user.

Hepatitis

Hepatitis is a serious inflammation of the liver caused by infection with any one of a number of hepatitis viruses. It can cause fever, fatigue, headaches, and jaundice, and it can eventually trigger liver failure and cancer. Hepatitis infection is spread through contact with the bodily fluids of an infected person, so people who inject drugs and share needles are at particular risk. When someone injects, traces of their blood remain on the needle. If he or she has hepatitis, someone else using the same needle will inject infected blood into his or her own bloodstream. Hepatitis infection can also be passed on by sexual intercourse.

Injecting
Injecting drug users may tie something tight around their arms to make a vein become prominent, allowing them to inject the drug.

Hepatitis B and hepatitis C are common among injecting drug users (IDUs), and it is estimated that between 60 and 70 percent of the world's IDUs are infected with the hepatitis C virus, while between 40 and 60 percent are thought to be infected with hepatitis B.

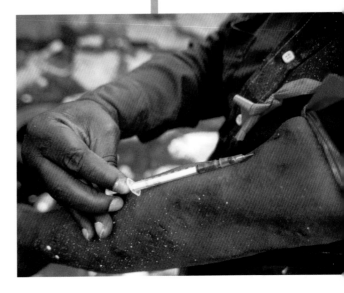

Tetanus

Tetanus is an infection that enters the body through the puncture wound left by the needle. It acts on the nerves that control muscle activity, causing muscle stiffness, headache, and fever. As the illness progresses, the muscles may go into painful spasms, and if the throat or chest is affected, breathing difficulties may occur and there is a risk of suffocation. Tetanus may kill if not treated quickly.

Collapsed veins

Repeated injecting can result in collapsed veins. Damage to some veins in an area means that blood is pumped there faster than the remaining veins can carry it away. So, for example, the arms, legs, hands, or feet may become swollen and puffy, turn a bluish color, and be cold to the touch. Where veins are damaged, there is insufficient blood flow to allow healing, and this damage is irreversible. The injection sites may become infected, causing boils or abscesses. Small scratches or knocks to the legs or feet are unable to heal properly and may become ulcerated. Ulcers are extremely painful open sores that can take months or even years to heal. If blood flow is severely restricted, areas of skin may even die, causing gangrene to set in. The affected parts may need to be amputated.

Another problem associated with collapsed veins is that the user soon runs out of veins in which to inject and resorts to injecting in other areas, including the groin, genitals, or even the eyeball.

Abscesses

Abscesses are inflamed, pus-filled areas of flesh. They are usually swollen and painful and may feel hot to the touch. Abscesses develop as a result of unhygienic injecting: bacteria on the skin enter the body through the puncture made by the needle and set up an infection.

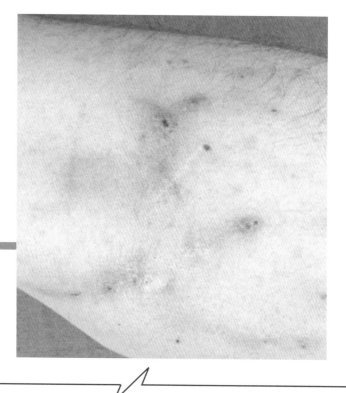

Irreversible damage
Scars left by injecting are likely to remain for life.

Skin problems

"Bad skin" is often associated with heroin use. It tends to be due more to the poor health and inadequate diet of the user than to the drug itself. Heroin users often appear pale and haggard-looking for the same reason.

HIV and AIDS

Like hepatitis viruses, the Human Immunodeficiency Virus (HIV) is carried in bodily fluids and so can be transmitted through sharing needles with an infected person and through sexual intercourse. HIV can lead to Acquired Immune Deficiency Syndrome (AIDS). HIV infection gradually breaks down the body's immune system, making the infected person more susceptible to a number of infections and to certain types of cancer. When someone develops certain diseases and cancers as a result of HIV infection, they are diagnosed as having AIDS. Some conditions that occur as a result of HIV infection can be treated, but at present there is no cure and no vaccine.

"You want to know who does heroin around here? Just take a look. You can tell the scag-heads easy enough—they're the ones who look like corpses covered in scabs." (Bernie, who stays in a shelter for young homeless men)

HIV and Needles

According to the British Medical Association, half of all people infected with HIV will develop AIDS within ten years and will die from a related condition. The number of people who have become infected through needle-sharing varies worldwide. In New York City alone, there are an estimated 100,000 needle users who are HIV-positive (this means that the HIV virus is present in their blood). In the United Kingdom, about 3,000 people are thought to have become infected in this way.

"When you're desperate, you just don't care"

Danny is 24 and has recently been told that he has full-blown AIDS. He is suffering from several illnesses, including cancer, and can no longer walk more than a few steps unaided.

"I don't know how long I've got," says Danny, "but put it this way: I'm not bothering to book a vacation next year." He laughs, but the laughter becomes a painful coughing fit and a nurse puts an oxygen mask over his face. After a few minutes, he continues, his voice weak and rasping: "I knew I was risking getting AIDS, but when you're desperate for a hit, you just don't care. You have to get the stuff into your veins somehow, and if that means sharing a needle, then that's what you do. You never think it'll happen to you, of course.

"I started injecting because smoking didn't give such a kick any more. I'd heard that shooting up gave you a fantastic high, and it did— but only the first time. After that, it was never as good, and in the end, I was only doing it to stop myself from feeling ill.

"By the time I admitted I was a junkie, it was too late. I was diagnosed as HIV-positive two years ago. Since then, I've been ill most of the time, in and out of the hospital. I'm not scared of dying, but I feel guilty for my mom and my sister. They get really upset when they visit, and my mom cries sometimes. I wish I hadn't been so stupid."

Heroin and pregnancy

If a woman uses heroin while pregnant, she is more likely to have a miscarriage (when the fetus dies in the early stages of pregnancy and is expelled by the body). There is also an increased risk of the baby being born too early. This is known as premature delivery, and it makes the baby more vulnerable to infection and more likely to have breathing difficulties and development problems.

"I went into labor early, but they said my baby was already dead, because of the heroin. I had to go through the labor and delivery anyway. It was horrible. I know it was my fault she died." (Gemma, age 17)

Babies born to heroin-addicted mothers are likely to be of low birth weight and tend to be in poor health generally—although this may be partly because of the mother's poor health and nutrition due to the lifestyle associated with heroin use, rather than to the heroin itself. The babies are also more at risk of Sudden Infant Death Syndrome (SIDS), and if their mothers have used heroin intravenously, they may be born HIV-positive.

A dangerous start

A baby born prematurely needs intensive care. Its immune system is not fully developed, and so infection is a great danger.

During pregnancy, heroin can cross from the mother's bloodstream, via the placenta (an organ in the womb), into the baby's bloodstream. This means that babies born to heroin-addicted mothers are born addicted and therefore experience painful and distressing withdrawal symptoms during the first few days of life.

Expectant mothers who are addicted to heroin are often treated with methadone (read more about this in Chapter 6). Although this can still result in the baby having some dependency, it is generally less harmful than heroin. Pregnant women should not stop using heroin suddenly and without medical supervision, since sudden withdrawal can be fatal to the fetus.

"I saw a documentary on TV, where this woman was a heroin addict and she had a baby who was addicted too. I think it died."
(Chloe, age 15)

The agony of a tiny baby

"I've been clean for over a year now. I'll never forget what it was like seeing Maisie in agony just after she was born. She just screamed and screamed, and whenever I went near her, she looked terrified. I didn't know what was wrong with her at first. Then a nurse told me that she was suffering from withdrawal. The nurse was horrible to me, calling me selfish and stupid, but I suppose I deserved it.

"When I was pregnant, I was just wrapped up in myself, hanging out with the others in the house where I lived and shooting up all the time. I had no contact with my family, and I never saw Maisie's dad again, so I didn't talk to anyone about my pregnancy. I didn't even see a doctor until I went into labor. I know it sounds crazy, but it really never occurred to me how much damage I might be doing to my baby. They said I was lucky she made it— lots of babies don't. I love Maisie so much. I'm really trying to make it up to her now."
(Hayley, age 18)

5 The Social Consequences
The End of Normal Life

Once people are in the grip of heroin addiction, it becomes increasingly difficult for them to continue with what we would regard as "normal" life— studying or working; having relationships with family, friends, and partners; taking care of their homes; looking after their health and appearance; and enjoying interests or hobbies. Before long, heroin becomes the most important thing in their lives. This is because addiction means that, if they do not get their regular dose of the drug, they begin to suffer withdrawal symptoms that can be extremely painful and distressing. The result is that they spend most of their time and energy on finding the next dose and, of course, the money to pay for it.

It is estimated that the average heroin habit costs between $170 and $500 a week. Although occasional users may hold down a job, people who become addicted will find it very difficult to work while coping with the physical effects of regular heroin use. Soon, therefore, users find they are spending considerably more on their heroin habit than they can earn or receive in welfare. They start to sell their large possessions. Once all the large items have gone, they sell smaller items, such as CDs and clothing— anything that will bring in a few dollars toward the next hit.

On the street
Many heroin users end up living on the street.

Once users have sold all their own possessions, they often move on to stealing, at first from family and friends, perhaps taking money from their parents' homes or taking small items that they can sell. They may even convince themselves that they are only "borrowing" and will replace what they have stolen later. They may move from this into burglary, robbery, fraud, or prostitution. It is often the case that heroin users who have never previously broken the law turn to crime as a way to fund their habit.

The long-term social cost

Researchers at the University of California carried out a study lasting more than 30 years. They found that long-term heroin use resulted in higher levels of health problems, premature death, criminal behavior and imprisonment, and reliance on welfare.

Nearly 600 male heroin addicts were monitored from the early 1960s through 1997. By that time, nearly half had died—a death rate of between 50 and 100 times higher than that among non–heroin users in the same age-range. The most common cause of death (21 percent) was accidental overdose. About 20 percent of deaths were due to suicide, murder, or accident. Most of the rest were due to liver disease, cancer, and heart disease.

Heroin and the family

Heroin can be at the root of breakdowns in relationships between couples, parents and children, siblings, and within the wider family. There is often a certain amount of deception and betrayal of trust involved in hiding and funding a heroin habit, and this causes problems within families. Parents may feel they can no longer leave their child alone in the house because he or she is likely to steal things. A wife or husband may feel they can never again trust a partner who has been lying.

"My brother's stuff was disappearing. He said he'd lent it to friends, but wouldn't say who. I knew he was selling it. Then he sold Mom's engagement ring —just after that, he admitted he was a heroin addict." (Bethann, age 16)

Also, the very nature of heroin addiction, a craving for the drug that becomes the focus of people's lives above all else, means that heroin users have neither the time nor the energy to contribute to a normal relationship with family, friends, or partners. Some people who are married to heroin users describe the drug as though it were an affair their spouse is having.

For the children of heroin addicts, life is even more dismal. Apart from financial hardship, which can result in malnutrition and general poor health, there is a strong likelihood that the children will not be properly cared for. Heroin addicts, as we have seen, soon become focused mainly on finding and paying for heroin. Therefore, although they may love their children, they may be unable to care for them. Children may face hunger, lack of personal care, illness due to living in unhygienic surroundings, and accidents resulting from being left unattended, either because the parent is out finding heroin or is in a heroin-induced stupor. There is also a risk of children accidentally taking heroin themselves or becoming infected with HIV or hepatitis if they come into contact with used syringes.

Looking away

Children whose parents are drug users may find strategies to cope with the distress it causes and the lifestyle it entails. Sadly, they may become used to the fact that their parents are not "there" for them.

Children of addicts also suffer socially. Addicts often lose their homes, which may mean that they end up living in shelters or even on the streets. In some cases, their children may be placed in foster care or be taken permanently into the care of the state.

Another problem is the continuing cycle of drug abuse. It is estimated that 70 percent of children with a parent who is addicted to drugs will become addicted themselves. This may be because they have inherited a tendency to addiction, although there is little research on this. It may also be because they become so used to the lifestyle that goes with addiction that they drift into patterns of behavior similar to that of their parents.

"It's hard deciding to take children away from their parents, but when you see kids going hungry, or having to call an ambulance because mommy's overdosed again, you have to consider putting them in care." (Julie, social worker)

"She cries for her mommy"

Lynne's daughter, Molly, is 25 and has been addicted to heroin since she was 18. Molly's little girl, Jasmine, is 6, and she now lives with Lynne.

"I thought things were getting better," says Lynne. "Molly was in a rehabilitation program. She said she was determined to succeed, for Jasmine's sake. But I could see it wasn't working. She was in a daze half the time. When I went to visit, I couldn't believe the state of her apartment. She'd sold all the furniture to pay for heroin, and even the little silver mug I bought Jasmine for her christening. She was embarrassed when I found out, and I know she feels bad, but she can't stop herself.

"One day, Jasmine saw me using a stock cube to make gravy. She said, 'I don't like stock soup. We have it all the time.' Molly had been feeding the child on stock cubes and hot water, and telling her it was soup! That's when I said Jasmine should come and live with me. It was heartbreaking to do that to my own daughter, to take her child away from her, but I couldn't watch my grandchild going hungry. I've begged Molly to get help, and she keeps promising that she will, soon. In the meantime, I hear Jasmine crying for her mommy, and I cry, too. For Jasmine, and for my daughter."

Prison

Drug use is a major problem in prisons in the United States. Strict drug laws in the United States have resulted in a huge increase in the prison population, which is now almost two million. It is estimated that about 60 percent of inmates are there for drug-related crimes. There are few studies in this area, so it is not possible to estimate the extent of heroin use specifically, but we do know that heroin addiction is a problem. Heroin is

Isolation

Someone whose parents are drug users is likely to try to keep it hidden. Doing so may make them seem unfriendly, and they may become isolated.

"I wish my mom and dad would stop taking heroin. We never have any money, and I'm too embarrassed to bring my friends home. When things are really bad, I have to live with my foster parents. They're nice, but I wish I could stay at my house." (Rhys, age 12)

Addiction can lead to misery and crime

Leah is eighteen and has been working as a prostitute for over a year.

"I'm not proud of what I do. I didn't even realize what I was getting into. I've been hooked on smack for a couple of years now, and it was getting harder and harder to find the cash—I spend about $350 a week. Anyway, one day, I was really desperate. I was feeling bad, shivering and pains and stuff, and then this guy said if I slept with him, he'd help me out. So I did. That happened a few times, and then he started introducing me to other guys who would pay me to do stuff, and I just sort of fell into it from there. It's a horrible way to survive, but I don't know what else to do. I've been raped twice—they just think you're worthless and that you deserve it. I've also been arrested. I'll get myself together one day, but I'm not sure how."

Drug crimes and penalties

Buying, selling, or using heroin is against the law. There are three main "drug" crimes: possession, supply, and possession with intent to supply. How these crimes are defined remains unclear, and the interpretation is up to the police and the courts. Even if someone gives a small amount of heroin to a friend and does not receive payment, this can still be seen as "supply" and carries stiff penalties. Penalties and laws can vary from state to state and vary widely from country to country.

Crime can lead to misery and addiction

"I was fine before I went inside. I used to smoke a bit of pot now and then, or take a few pills. But I would never have touched heroin. Then I got arrested for stealing. It was only a few things from work—video recorders, stereos, that sort of thing. But it was a second offense, so the judge sent me to prison. I got out after a year, but by that time, I was hooked. Heroin's the easiest drug to get in prison, and you have to do something to relieve the boredom. I don't know how it gets in, but there's no shortage.

"Anyway, since I came out, my wife, Janine, has taken our little boy, Thomas—he's two—and moved back to her mom's. She says she doesn't want to see me any more, and she won't let me see Thomas, because she doesn't trust me not to shoot up while he's there. I swore I wouldn't, but if I'm totally honest, I probably would, if I needed it. We've lost our apartment, and at the moment, I'm sleeping on friends' floors—my mom wouldn't have me back because of the drugs. And I'm losing friends fast. Even my best friend from school said he doesn't want anything to do with me until I'm off the junk. Trouble is, what's the point of coming off it? I've got no job, no home, no wife, and no kid, and my mom won't speak to me. What else is there?"

(Nick, age 23)

In jail

Heroin users may end up in jail for possessing or supplying the drug, or for crimes committed in order to obtain it. However, some people say that it was in jail that they started using heroin.

also the most widely used drug in prisons in the United Kingdom. It has been suggested that random drug testing within prisons may have contributed to the problem. If prisoners are found to have drugs in their system, they face punishments ranging from enforced segregation to having days added to their sentence, so obviously they are eager to avoid being caught. Heroin only stays in the body for about 78 hours, whereas marijuana, which many argue is less harmful and less addictive, can still be found in the body after four weeks. Drug tests are therefore much less likely to pick up heroin than they are to find traces of marijuana, and this has made heroin the new "drug of choice" in prisons.

Since needles are hard to come by in prison, injecting or tattooing (a popular pastime in prison) with used needles is common among inmates, and this has led to increased rates of HIV and hepatitis. There are calls for tighter security, to prevent drugs from getting into prisons, and more treatment programs that help inmates suffering from addiction.

Smuggling

Heroin is sometimes hidden in vehicles and brought into the country via ferries, or it may be concealed in luggage, clothing, or, in some cases, the carrier's stomach, after being swallowed (see Chapter 2). In recent years there has been much publicity about people being talked into acting as "mules" to smuggle fairly small amounts of heroin into a country. Young people in particular may be approached while on vacation and offered large amounts of money for what seems like "easy" work. The idea is that ordinary vacationers are less likely to cause suspicion when they go through customs, so they simply conceal the drug in their suitcases, carry it through customs, and then receive payment when they hand it over to the "contact," who will meet them after their return. Due to recent world events, airport security is tighter than ever, so the drug smugglers may have to rethink their strategy. It may be that, as well as reducing the risk of a terrorist attack, increased security will reduce the amount of illegal drugs being smuggled into countries such as the United States.

The penalties for smuggling heroin are severe: up to life imprisonment or, in some countries, the death penalty.

Apart from the risk of being caught, heroin carried inside the body is extremely dangerous, and people have died as a result of the packages bursting inside their stomachs.

Guns, gangs, and "gangsta rap"

There have always been links between drugs and violent crime, but the use of guns in drug-related crime is on the increase, with dealers battling it out on the streets over who is "in charge" of certain areas—so-called "turf wars." Drug-related gang crime, often involving teenagers as young as fourteen, is also on the increase, both in the United States and in the United Kingdom. These gangs are more common in low-income or deprived areas and are often made up of young people who have fallen outside of the "normal" social system—for example, those who do not have a family home, whose home life is unhappy, who have serious problems at school or do not attend school, or who have a criminal record. For teenagers from an unstable, unhappy, or abusive background, being a member of a gang can seem attractive, almost like a substitute family.

Customs search
Customs officers have specially trained dogs to help them find drugs concealed in people's luggage.

Research suggests that many gang members already have a criminal background, often involving theft, fraud, drug dealing, and violent crime. The activities of gangs vary enormously, but drug dealing is common and often results in violence between rival gangs. Police believe that, in some areas, youth gangs may be linked with adult criminal organizations that are involved in drug smuggling.

There has been much discussion recently about "gangsta rap" and whether the lyrics, which often dwell on violence and drug use, actually contribute to the rise in the use of heroin and other hard drugs. While it is true that some of these rap lyrics do seem to promote heroin, it is unlikely that they are directly responsible for the recent rise in use of the drug, particularly since pro-heroin lyrics have been around since the 1970s. However, some people argue that, if young people continually hear songs talking about and praising drug use as a "cool" or even "okay" thing to do, they may soon come to think of drug use as normal.

Drug debate
People have differing views about whether rap lyrics about drugs inspire people to try heroin.

6 Prevention and Treatment
A Heroin-Free Future

Education and prevention

One of the best ways to reduce the devastation caused by heroin addiction is to prevent more people from trying the drug in the future. Hopefully, this can be achieved by improved drug education. Most people agree that drug education is essential, but there is debate about what form it should take.

"Shock horror" tactics have sometimes been used in an attempt to frighten people away from using drugs. The parents of a 21-year-old British student who died after injecting heroin wanted pictures of their daughter's body to be used as "a warning to others" about the dangers of heroin. Rachel Whitear's body was found on the floor of her apartment three days after she died. Her flesh was bruised, swollen, and discolored, and she was still clutching the syringe she had used to inject herself with heroin. The harrowing picture has been included in an educational video—a move welcomed by the parents of other young people who have died from drug abuse.

However, research from around the world suggests that shock tactics do not work. Drug education professionals feel that the best

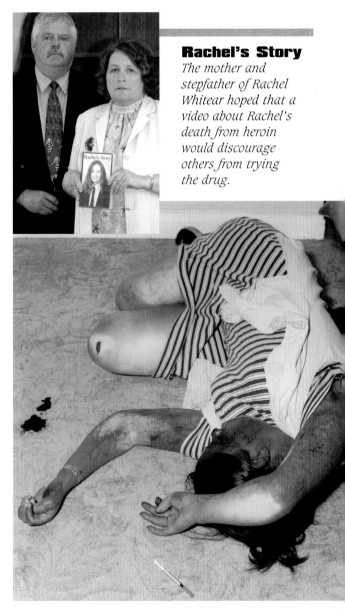

Rachel's Story
The mother and stepfather of Rachel Whitear hoped that a video about Rachel's death from heroin would discourage others from trying the drug.

way to teach children and teenagers about drugs is to give them plenty of information and to encourage open discussion.

Many organizations and pressure groups campaign for an improved approach. Some suggest that children should receive regular drug education from the age of five. Experts agree that discussion about drugs should be part of all-around health education, at school and at home, and that it should also involve building up children's personalities and self-esteem. The idea is that, as you get older, this will give you the confidence to know what you think about the issues and the social skills to express your opinions. Then, if you are faced with a situation in which you are under pressure to behave in a way that might be dangerous, you will be able to say, "Thanks, but this isn't for me."

Parents
Talking honestly with your parents about drugs can help you make good choices.

Lee, an ex-user, helps others

"Where I grew up, most kids were in trouble with the police by the time they were thirteen. There was no point in going to school—you knew you'd never get a job— so we just used to steal stuff, partly for the money, but mainly out of boredom.

"We lived in a high-rise building in one of the roughest housing projects in the country. All the kids in the project did drugs. You'd start off sniffing aerosols, move on to marijuana, and before long, heroin or crack. My mom's boyfriend, Mick, used heroin. He gave me some on my sixteenth birthday, for a "treat," and it felt really grown-up. My mom got mad at us, but we never cared.

"By the time I was eighteen, I was an addict. Mick died of an overdose a few years later, and after that my mom begged me to get treatment. I tried a few times, but I kept dropping out. Then one day I was talking to a guy at the needle exchange and I thought, 'He's right. This is stupid.' So I got myself on a methadone program and, with lots of support, I got off heroin.

"I've been clean for four years, and for the last two, I've been working for a drug center. I'm training to be a qualified drug counselor, and I think my experience helps—I know where they're coming from, what they're going through, and so on. It's rewarding work and it's really turned my life around."
(Lee, age 25)

A social problem

A lot of research suggests that heroin use is more common in deprived areas. Various studies show that heroin use was highest in the poorest households, for the age groups between 16 and 29, and that the use of any drug was higher among those who were unemployed. In a study of eleven-to fifteen-year-olds, drug use was highest among those who felt they would not do as well in school as they thought other people expected them to. Heroin use was more common in sixteen-to nineteen-year-olds who had dropped out of high school.

People from areas where financial hardship is common are said to be "socially excluded." This means that they tend

Environment
It seems that heroin use is more common in deprived environments.

to have fewer opportunities for education, employment, health care, and housing. Crime is more prevalent in these areas for obvious reasons. Living in conditions such as these often leads to frustration, misery, and depression, and it may be that this is when some people turn to drugs. As the research suggests, the use of heroin and other drugs is more common in these areas.

Many people believe that changes in society to improve education, employment prospects, and housing would help reduce social exclusion and therefore reduce heroin use. However, although there is clearly a link between heroin use and social exclusion, others argue that it is difficult to know which way we should look at things: does social exclusion cause people to turn to drugs, or is it that drug use leads to social exclusion?

Costs

It is extremely difficult to estimate the cost of heroin addiction, but in the United States, the cost has been estimated at more than $20 billion. A recent study in the United Kingdom showed the cost of policing drug misuse and providing treatment to be $5 to 6.7 billion. Research suggests that between 50 and 70 percent of all recorded crime is in some way drug-related.

How can heroin addiction be treated?

As we have seen, addiction to heroin can ruin lives in terms of health, relationships, employment, and housing. But addiction can be treated, and the sooner treatment begins, the more likely the user is to recover and stay off heroin. Since heroin controls people's lives, becoming the only thing they are interested in, it can be difficult to get them to seek treatment, and so it may be some time before they get the help they need. Some people do seek treatment themselves, maybe because they realize their heroin use is out of control or because of associated health problems.

"This may sound stupid, but getting sent to jail was the best thing for me. Outside, I'd never have gone to a treatment program, but inside, I got to think about my life and thought, 'Why not?' Once I got started, I really wanted to succeed." (Jay, age 19)

Sometimes it is the family doctor who suggests treatment. Often, users are referred to treatment after ending up in a hospital emergency room after an accidental overdose. In some cases, a shelter for the homeless or a local drug counseling service puts users in touch with a treatment center. Many others come through the criminal justice system, with treatment being a condition of their release or a part of their sentence. Many believe there should be more treatment programs offered in prisons.

Getting her life back—with help

"I only started going to the Project because someone told me they can help you get free heroin, but that turned out not to be true. I've kept on going though, because they're really nice and they don't judge you. There's lots of information about different types of treatment and stuff, but they don't force you. I said I didn't want treatment at first, but I've been talking to Lee quite a lot, and he's just about convinced me.

"I would like to get off it, but I suppose I'm a little scared. I can't remember what it was like to get through the day without heroin, but Lee says you can get back to how you were before, and that you don't have to do anything you don't want to. I guess he knows what he's talking about, so I've agreed to be referred to a treatment center. Lee's going to come with me for my first appointment. In a way, it's quite exciting—it means I might actually get my life back." (Risana, age 17)

Getting off heroin is very difficult for someone who has become dependent. First, as the last dose of heroin leaves the body, users start to experience unpleasant and painful withdrawal symptoms. They know that taking heroin will relieve those symptoms, and therefore long for more heroin (this is called "craving"). One method of treatment is to prescribe a controlled dose of another drug—a heroin substitute—that will relieve the withdrawal symptoms.

But even when the cravings and withdrawal symptoms are relieved, users often find it difficult to adjust to a heroin-free way of life. This usually involves mixing with different people and getting used to new daily routines, including new patterns of eating, sleeping, and exercise. Because addicts have become dependent both on the drug itself and on a heroin user's lifestyle, experts believe that the most effective approach is a combination of medical treatment and counseling or behavior therapy. Recovering from physical addiction and learning to live a heroin-free life is called "rehabilitation," and a combination of treatments and

Withdrawal

These two men were photographed at a "Reeducation Center" for heroin addicts in Hanoi, Vietnam. One is reassuring the other as he suffers the symptoms of withdrawal from the drug.

therapy or counseling to help someone achieve this is often called a "rehabilitation program."

Heroin addiction is described by professionals in the field as "a chronic, relapsing condition." This means that people may have to make several attempts to get off heroin before they succeed. Roughly half of those who begin a treatment program will drop out, and of those who complete the program, about half will still be "clean" (off heroin) two years later.

Methadone

The human-made opiate methadone is probably the most widely used treatment for heroin addiction. It works as a substitute for heroin by relieving withdrawal symptoms and suppressing cravings, without producing the heroin "high." Some people argue that it merely creates another addiction, and it is true that patients can become dependent on it. However, the amount taken may be gradually decreased ("methadone reduction"). Even if the dosage remains the same ("methadone maintenance"), it is safer than heroin.

"It's great when someone says, 'Thanks for your help, Martha. I'll never use heroin again.' Some do, of course, but then we'll help them to get off it again." (Martha, a nurse at a rehabilitation clinic)

Like heroin, methadone is a drug with a high street value, so it is usually given at the clinic, in the form of a liquid medicine that only needs to be taken once a day. Correct dosage is vital—if the dose does not relieve the withdrawal symptoms, patients are likely to go back to heroin to relieve their discomfort. This sets up the craving again, and users are back in the cycle of addiction.

Studies carried out in the United States show that between 65 and 85 percent of people on methadone stay in treatment for a year or more, and the longer they do so, the better the outcome. Research shows that, in general, methadone patients are less likely to be involved in crime and more likely to be employed during treatment. There is also a considerable improvement in health and nutrition.

Heroin on prescription

In some countries when an addict has a high level of dependency, and other forms of treatment have not worked, doctors sometimes may decide to treat people by prescribing heroin. This is the only way in which heroin may be used legally. (Heroin cannot be prescribed in the United States, however.) Heroin prescribing is controversial, with some doctors suggesting that it merely keeps people addicted. The advantage is that, although users remain addicted, the amount of heroin they use and its purity can be controlled. People can also be given clean needles and syringes, reducing the risk of harm through injecting street heroin.

People on heroin prescriptions would be treated in a residential clinic or as hospital inpatients, or they would have to visit the clinic each time they needed an injection— possibly three to four times a day. Only very rarely, once their condition had been stable for some time, would they be allowed to use prescription heroin at home.

Some law enforcement officials are in favor of more widespread prescribing, arguing that it may reduce crime. Health workers also point out that prescribing heroin keeps the user in touch with treatment services, so there may be a possibility of trying other forms of treatment again later.

Detoxification

This is a process in which the patient undergoes medically supervised withdrawal, either as an inpatient or as an outpatient. Usually medication is used to relieve withdrawal symptoms, although it is possible to detox without medication. The idea is that once all traces of heroin have left the body, only the psychological addiction needs to be dealt with.

Counseling

There are some drug counselors to whom people can go on a "drop-in" basis, when they want help and advice. There

Needle exchange programs

Needle exchange programs collect and dispose of used syringes and needles and offer new sterile syringes and needles in exchange. This reduces the risk of HIV, hepatitis, and other blood-borne infections being spread among injecting drug users.

The programs may also offer advice and counseling on drug and other health, social, and welfare problems, as well as providing access or referral to other treatment services. Needle exchange programs are also a good way to get information to users about available treatment and services.

Some people argue that providing clean needles in this way increases intravenous drug use, though there is no evidence to support this. Research from several countries suggests that the programs are effective and can significantly reduce risky behavior.

is also a more formal, structured type of counseling in which treatment plans are made, goals are set, and regular reviews are carried out. Counseling may be offered as part of a "package," including medication, education and/or training, and management of other health problems. Studies show that those who have quality counseling are less likely to go back to heroin after treatment.

Structured or full-time outpatient programs

These programs offer an intensive form of rehabilitation that lasts about twelve to sixteen weeks. They are often

Advice on the street
Needle exchange workers meet the heroin users in their own environment and may be able to encourage them to get treatment for their addiction.

recommended in law courts as part of a "sentencing order." If someone's crime appears to be linked to his or her heroin addiction, the judge may make the sentence conditional on the addict attending one of these programs. Attendance is usually full-time, similar to college or working hours.

Programs may focus on beating addiction or on education or vocational training. They may also be targeted at particular types of heroin users, such as criminals. Many offer a combination of approaches. The aim is to provide access to information and advice and to help users develop other areas of their lives so that they can move back into society.

Where does treatment take place?

⊛ Users unable to manage their own treatment without constant support are treated as inpatients, supervised by medical staff in a hospital or specialist clinic. Sometimes a user undergoes detoxification in the hospital and then has other forms of treatment as an outpatient.

⊛ Some users are treated at a residential center other than a hospital or clinic. There may be medical supervision, but as part of a wider rehabilitation program. A residential center creates a "structured environment" in which users learn to live without heroin. When the user returns home, to his or her "real environment," it might be difficult not to return to old habits associated with heroin use.

⊛ Many people go for treatment as outpatients. To start with, they visit the clinic every day to be given their medication. Later they may be able to move to using the medication at home. They may also go for counseling, sometimes over a period of several months.

How long does it take?

How long treatment takes depends on many factors, including how dependent the person is, what treatment is being used, where it is carried out, how much the person wants to get off heroin, and whether the person is a "polydrug user"—someone who uses more than one drug at a time. Research suggests that the majority of heroin addicts are polydrug users. On average, an inpatient detoxification program, using medication to reduce withdrawal symptoms, takes between two and seven weeks.

What works?

Different approaches suit different people, but, in general, a combination of treatments is thought to be most effective for heroin addiction. Few studies have been completed on the effectiveness of the various forms of treatment, but those that are available tend to show a greater success rate among people undergoing inpatient or residential treatment.

Counseling
Talking to a drug counselor is a major part of recovering from addiction.

Heroin addiction is a cruel affliction that affects not only the individual, but also his or her family and friends and society in general. Not only does it cause terrible illness, pain, and death, but it takes away all sense of purpose and any sense of true happiness from those who become dependent. However, people can and do recover. Recovery can be difficult and traumatic, and the person may slip back several times before finally succeeding in becoming "clean." Those who have pulled themselves out of the cycle of addiction talk of being "reborn" and of being given "another chance at life."

"When we saw Natasha in that hospital bed last year, her arms covered with track marks, her eyes sunken and hollow, we really didn't think she'd be with us today. We are so thankful that she got the help she needed, and that we have our daughter back."

Glossary

addiction — dependence on a drug

analgesic — painkilling substance. There are many legal analgesics on the market—for example, ibuprofen, and aspirin.

asphyxiation — suffocation due to a blockage in the airways

central nervous system — brain and spinal cord, where "messages" move from the brain to various parts of the body

chronic — long-lasting or frequently recurring, such as in illness

codeine — analgesic drug derived from opium

coma — deep unconsciousness caused by injury, illness, or poison

compulsive — needing, or feeling compelled, to do something. This is the sort of behavior that occurs with addiction.

criminal justice system — system through which someone can be arrested, prosecuted, sentenced, and imprisoned

Demerol — human-made opiate that produces a "rush"

dependence — powerful physical and/or psychological craving for a substance

detoxification — process of allowing the body to rid itself of toxins

dopamine — brain chemical that regulates emotion

endorphins — "feel-good" chemicals that occur naturally in the brain

euphoria — intense feeling of pleasure, well-being, or excitement

fix — slang term for a dose of heroin

gangrene — when body tissue dies due to bacterial infection or loss of blood supply

hepatitis — inflammation of the liver

hookah — pipe used to smoke opium

immune system — body's natural defense system, responsible for protection against and fighting off infection

intravenous — into the vein (as in an injection)

junkie — slang term for a heroin addict

labor — when a pregnant woman is "in labor" it means that the process of childbirth has started. The labor describes the period from the first contraction (tightening) of the uterus until the baby is actually born.

laudanum — mixture of opium, alcohol, and spices, popular in the 19th century and used recreationally by many people, particularly artists and writers

malnutrition — state of being undernourished as a result of a poor or inadequate diet

methadone — human-made opiate that is used in treatment as a substitute for heroin. It is addictive.

morphine	analgesic drug derived from opium
narcotic	drug that causes extreme drowsiness
narcotism	state of being sleepy or drowsy as a result of taking narcotic drugs
opiates	group of drugs that are derived from opium, including synthetic opiates, which have similar effects
opioids	more general term for opiates
opium	sticky substance that comes from the opium poppy
polydrug user	someone who uses more than one drug
rehabilitation	process of recovering—physically, psychologically, and socially—from addiction
relapse	return of an illness or a condition such as addiction after apparent recovery

rush	term used to describe the sudden feeling of euphoria experienced by a heroin user
Sudden Infant Death Syndrome (SIDS)	sudden unexpected death of a baby for no apparent reason
synthetic	human-made, not a natural product
syringe	glass or plastic cylinder with a needle attached for injecting heroin (or other substances) into the body
tolerance	physical state of adjustment to the presence of a substance, meaning that more is then needed to create a reaction
withdrawal	process of getting off an addictive substance

Resources

Organizations

Center for Substance Abuse Prevention
5600 Fishers Lane, Rockwall II
Rockville, MD 20857
(310) 443-0365
www.samhsa.gov

Child Welfare League of America
440 First Street NW
Washington, D.C. 20001
(202) 638-2952
www.cwla.org

DARE America
(drug abuse resistance and education)
P.O. Box 775
Dumfries, VA 22026
(703) 860-3273
www.dare.com

Narcotics Anonymous
P.O. Box 9999
Van Nuys, CA 91409
(800) 467-7314
www.na.org

Books

Connolly, Sean. *Heroin.* Chicago: Heinemann, 2000.

Cothran, Helen. *Heroin.* Farmington Hills, Mich.: Gale Group, 2001.

Westcott, Patty. *Why Do People Take Drugs?* Chicago: Raintree, 2001.

Index